The Equalizing Jokebook

poems by

Rose Novick

Finishing Line Press
Georgetown, Kentucky

The Equalizing Jokebook

Copyright © 2023 by Rose Novick
ISBN 979-8-88838-159-5 First Edition
All rights reserved under International and Pan-American Copyright Conventions. No part of this book may be reproduced in any manner whatsoever without written permission from the publisher, except in the case of brief quotations embodied in critical articles and reviews.

ACKNOWLEDGMENTS

Poems in this book have previously appeared in the following venues:

The American Journal of Poetry: Woods; Haibun
Antiphon: (It appears crooked, that half-submerged)
Black Telephone Mag: Sonnet (FELICITY)
Book XI: Row, Row, Row…; (The deathless poem will be made of words)
Dunes Review: Low Tide; Postlude
Nothing in the Rulebook: Poem for John Ashbery; Magpie; Entering & Breaking; Flit
Notre Dame Review: Fleeing Ghost; Stalker
The Raintown Review: Free-Floating Clouds
Sequestrum: Sonnet ("Listen…"); "So priketh hem Nature in hir corages"; Ephemera

Publisher: Leah Huete de Maines
Editor: Christen Kincaid
Cover Art: Mel Andrews
Author Photo: Mel Andrews
Cover Design: Elizabeth Maines McCleavy

Order online: www.finishinglinepress.com
also available on amazon.com

Author inquiries and mail orders:
Finishing Line Press
P. O. Box 1626
Georgetown, Kentucky 40324
U. S. A.

Table of Contents

Its name is Kun 1
(The deathless poem will be made of words) 2
Polykleitos 3
Magpie 4
Rain 5
Sonnet 6
O the mind, mind has mountains 7
Xenophanes 8
Pindaric 9
Low Tide 10
Afterwards, I read Wang Wei 11
Scene 12
Woods 14
Sonnet 15
From the perspective of an emperor penguin chick… 16
The Cat is On the Mat 17
(Epicurus, you once described the gods) 18
Fleeing Ghost 19
Fell 20
Anepikrita 21
Nil mortalibus ardui est 23
Row, Row, Row. 24
Choose wisely 25
Mushrooms springing up in dampness 26
Poem for John Ashbery 27
Crane Collapse 28
Sprung 29
Knowing better 30
Haibun 31
Tangled Weeds 32
Detachment 33
Sonnet 34
"So priketh hem Nature in hir corages" 35
Ephemera 36
Sonnet 37
(The bottlebrushes tongue the air) 38
Heraclitus 39
Flit 41

Nothing Doing 43
Red Song 44
Dialogue 45
Look, man, here's the thing… 46
Canon 47
Entering & Breaking 48
Stalker 49
Pindaric 50
On the bottom, in blue, a painted fish 51
(It appears crooked, that half-submerged) 52
Free-Floating Clouds 54
Frogs in Artificial Light 55
Going 56

The Equalizing Jokebook is a record of curiosities. Its joke runs: "When the Peng migrates to the southern deep, it strikes the water for 3000 li. Spiraling on a cyclone, it rises 90000 li, departing on the midyear's breath."

—Zhuangzi

Orectic whir of whirling web
Contrived to captivate the fly,
Arachnid then imbibing death,
For animals by living die—

Don't peer like that with leery eye,
Spider! but go on, please, partake.
Didn't you know what doses make?

Preface

In the work's body, the person disappears; in its preface (I say incautiously, over Nāgasena's objections), the person remains to be found; thus no book should be released into this world without a preface.

This may seem strange to say about a book of poetry which, if it is to be slotted into any existing tradition, can only be regarded as confessional. But we often mislead ourselves with appearances, as any half-submerged stick will gladly inform you. In what follows, I am nowhere to be found, *I have lost **me**.* 今者吾喪我.

Today the Wabash, so recently overflowing, is receding back within its bounds, flotsam crowding its muddy banks, a tire sunk in ice. Pigeons leap from power lines and streetlamps, sinking toward the bridge below, then sink further still and pass beneath it, where to, I can't discern. In their silence, they seem to laugh at the cramped grey field above them, water clinging to the air's impurities and obscuring the sky's true color. In all laughter there is something of misunderstanding. Just this is what is lovable in laughter, for only by such reckless leaps do we span the gulf between us.

Master Hui, the greatest debater in ancient China, received from the King of Wei the seeds of a great gourd. This gourd was truly enormous, so enormous it could be used neither as a vessel nor as a scoop. What a shame Hui was so stupid when it came to big and useless things! He could not even think to make of his gourd a boat with which to float aimlessly to nowhere in particular. Among the poets and their champions today are so many Huis, convinced that poetry is (once again? at last?) necessary, now that the world is *sunken in mire*. I do not care for these solemn words. This little book is useless. Why not take a nap with it under a large and ugly tree, and converse with me in your dreams?

Many friends have, in their various ways, helped to see this through to abandonment; among these, I wish to single out Tim, Katie, Drew, Eden, Risa, Liam, Mat, and Andrew, to whom I owe especial gratitude.

The Equalizing Jokebook is dedicated to Yujing, with whom I changed.

Pittsburgh • Halifax • Lafayette • Seattle
2016-2020

Its name is Kun

Between them floated words, but to the Peng
    they were not words,
    they were haze.

        Consider, though, our lives, each moment strung
           like beads on wire,
           only—there is no wire.

Each mote of sense, invisible from such
    a height, formed a free surface
    in the pre-dawn air.

        I see your meaning—yes, it is too much
           to ask of wire—
           that's why we're always diffusing.

Already fog began to coalesce
    around this detritus,
    one droplet per word.

        You understand: I ask for nothing less
           than unity,
           and I'm frustrated, every time.

The Peng turned south and looked below: a blur
    of definition,
    silent, unmoving.

        Is wind enough? The fog begins to stir
           and move as one mass, although within
           it's churning…

By then the wind had gone, and the sun hung
    in an empty sky. Below,
    a mushroom sprouted, rank.

(The deathless poem will be made of words)

The deathless poem will be made of words,
and those words of letters, and those letters,
    in their turn, of indelible
    atoms suitably mixed
with void. There is the trouble, the void,
the emptiness that leaves room
    for motion. Give an atom
    room and it will swerve,
unpredictably. It may
not seem like much, a single atom
    swerving, but it compounds
    faster than you'd think.
That is why nothing fashioned from matter
lasts forever, not even the goddess
    who has so kindly given
    me these few words.
Do not be afraid, Felicity.
Death is nothing to us—nothing.

Polykleitos

Little by little, perfection creeps in,
a conspiracy of many numbers
reckoning, unheeded, among themselves.
    Soon—but not yet: the unkind
rattle of a bronze spear sends scurrying
some doryphore before Doryphoros
to wash, dismally, the flecks from his hands—
    soon I will burst in to find
what my hands have done. Standing before you,
glancing spearward, my body feels itself
misshapen. Please, just let me go. I am
    nobody. Pay me no mind.

Magpie

She works her fingers into an old stump,
down to the soft splinters, the harmless pricks
that goad no more, that turn to pulp beneath
persuasive hands.   She runs her fingers over
a stone, dwells on its round perfection, long
in birth and long in death, a moment etched
on a compendium of etchings.
                                She rakes
her fingers through a fire's corpse, ashes
bending to her figurations, lines
that speak her whim, furrows in gray that shade
her whorls.   She does not own these dreams. They cackle
across her synapses as she, echo
of their cachinnation, rises, leaves—
a flash of white and black caught hazily
through branches flush with needles. Thick, the air.
Breathe in. Again, more deeply. Smells like rain.

Rain

sodden, the sky that with
    skulk and

falter alleges its
    presence

overhead finds in the
    muffled

smur of the heavens with-
    in the

murmurs of concord with
    downfall

Sonnet

       Listen: you can hear
   the silent thunder gathering
before the clouds unload the loud, rude ring
       that stupefies the ear.

       Not yet insensate, here
   in the slurred rain, you feel each thing
that cannot be becoming, thickening
       from nothing, drawing near.

       What world is this, that streams
   with solid fog? What empty glut
       of all just as it seems?

       And, when real thunder fills
   the sky, and these things vanish—what?
       It is your mind that stills.

O the mind, mind has mountains

```
            The words bubble
              out of nothing
                pop    and scatter
              droplets    no longer full
                of air    no longer bound
              tensely    around an empty
              center     They freeze      held
            together   in a large mass     slowly
          pushing aside the mountains     erasing
        the mineral vestiges     of past life    grinding
          into shapeless dust      their forms      but slowly
            slowly    The poem      is a claw      that rakes
    the mind      moves it       this way       and that way
    seeking     in intricacies magnified      and multiplied
    seeking      in transient chasms        that swallow the traveler
        chasms      in which are lost      the great bulk      of events
          seeking        the silence       that resides        in the hearts
             of dwindling things        the emptiness       that coalesces
                around change          until it almost         feels solid
              Our footsteps      are reluctant          unwilling
                to trust the gripless surface          halting
                  before imagined crevasses         spaces
                    beckoning us to our fall       spaces
                      we feel we've crossed       before
                        The poem     is a forbidding
                           terrain        a glacier
                             in the     gathering
                                      blaze
```

Xenophanes

(I)

The sun is composed of ignited clouds,
And through its warmth it forms the clouds.

Who can find a beginning to this?
Everything cycles without beginning.

The sea exhales, and there is wind;
The wind drives waves across the sea.

Who can discover an end to this?
Everything cycles without end.

We are a mixture of earth and water.
Earth and water together are mud.

Who can find the logic of this?
Truly our thoughts fall short of the god's.

(II)

In Syracuse, impressions of fish.
In the mountains, shells within the rocks.

These things bespeak an age of mud,
When earth was softer than we know.

Even now, the sea is rising,
The earth dissolving in the moist.

After destruction, new creation:
Many and varied forms of mud.

Cycles—yes, a comforting notion,
But in each cycle, cataclysm.

Who can discover an escape from this?
The age of mud—who can escape it?

Pindaric

for Creüsa

Felicity, it is not you whose absence
the turbid Fates decreed. Then show yourself:
unclench my tongue, rigorous from disuse.
Pour from my mouth a song to soothe the air
that seethes with grief, that rends itself to mourn
Creüsa, wife who followed far behind,
woman who vanished, wraithlike, into night.

How did it happen? I imagine it
like this: Aeneas, Iulus, and Anchises
led the way. Trailing, as her husband bid,
Creüsa was one moment there, one moment
not. It was not Death, the laggard god,
who took her life. He came, but she was gone
already, faded by her own resolve.

She glimpsed her future as impediment—
that was enough to sway her. Silently,
she grasped Aeneas' want, saw Dido and
Lavinia. She saw one other, too:
a stranger's face.— There is a void where she
once was. I live within Creüsa's hollow:
from here I watch proud Ilium in flames.

Low Tide

   Its vacillations bulging
  shoreward, toward the turmoil of contact,
the froth of boundary, the ocean groaned
   with elation or with rage.

   And though its leavings teemed,
  they filled the kelp-lined pools with a substance
unfathomably clear, calm, and untroubled.
   Still, the ocean foamed.

   Only, the meaning got twisted,
  and no one could tell what it wanted to say.
Try as they might, none could decipher the spray
   erupting where the rocks resisted.

   We stayed there far too long—
   barnacles that guessed wrong.

Afterwards, I read Wang Wei

The full weight of error rests
on the earth, mingles with the remnants

of yesterday's snowfall, its black slush.
Asphalt duly salted and clear,

takeoff goes smoothly: words full of stillness
are corpses in my hands. The full

weight of error rests in the aisle,
threads through the whiteblue carpet. Something

tugs on the thread that raises hand
to forehead, what, I don't know, I'm tired.

The plane lands. The light brown earth
shows through the lollygagging snow.

Scene

I'd like to remember something, I'm not sure what.
I'm not even sure it's really remembering,
This re-creation of old longings: that time
In Russia, for example, when I watched
As smoke rose from a brick cigarette,
Brilliantly backlit by the rising sun.
But that was lifetimes ago, and I'm still young.

Or else this morning, in Pittsburgh. But the thread
Goes back far, too far, that the gods use to ravel
Clouds into people. And so we trail the wisps
Of homes we never had, and these distend
The cirrus that we're not, not really. Drop
Your needle through me, Vulcan—I'll not feel
The hole. But now the wind is picking up.

I was saying, about Russia… A cloud
Shields the sun, seeking story in shadow,
The meanings vouchsafed in its deformations,
The doodles of a darkened landscape. But
The marks are not transmissible. What's more,
The ground is drab, a plain of lone and level
Snow. Assuredly, there is no plot.

Near the horizon, a yarn begins to emerge,
But an old one, from which most pages are
Now lost. We call it "Seasons" or "The Year"
Or, sometimes, "Allegory", this tale of trees
Shedding their leaves, leaving behind those nubs
That serve me now as permanent reminders
Of errors I can never not have made.

The problem, I suppose, is that clouds lack
For gravity, not totally, to be sure,
But their size outstrips their mass. You know
How the formula goes. Or else it's that Vulcan never
Took his sewing seriously, always

Scampering off to the forge. Meaning: I'd like
To rest here, but I keep falling through, to the trees.

Among these, a failure of imagination:
I can only ever envision Russia
Flat, and gelid: all Siberia,
Which I imagine also in this way.
This waste I call my home, ancestrally—
Difficult terrain in which to locate
Biography. I'm hunting a white thread.

Apologies if I seem scattersouled.
For some time now, I've been envious of orange,
Of the dazzle of sun on diffusing smoke,
Its shadowy vanguard promising hidden riches
Even as it vanished. Of this, no more,
Though I can see the cigarette still fuming,
Exhausted phantoms fading into gauze.

Woods

Hidden here, nearly lost in undergrowth,
are the remnants of a wall, its smooth stones
scabbed with lichens, driven apart by vines.
Mostly it stands, but here a fallen tree
has severed it into unequal portions
and now lies in a pool of its gray blood.
Beneath the spattered stones, larvae are carving
out a soft existence. It is the charm
of this place that you may watch this furious
yet slow repurposing, this fructuous rot.

And what about the tree? The story here
is much the same: the living eat the dead
and die. Craneflies and spiders now reside
behind its wall of roots, as scalycaps
convert its trunk to loam. Peel back the bark
that feebly guards this soft religion: you
will encounter centipedes. Pick one up: you
will be aware of your finger for hours to come.
Yes, isn't it a comfort to hear old truths,
the same as ever, in unfamiliar words?

Sonnet

It no doubt seems an inopportune time
to discourse on metaphysics, what with the flies
not yet arrived to lay their eggs, the ants
not yet removing bits for their secret but guessable
purposes. *Too soon* shrills the general cry.
Nevertheless—
                 This squirrel here is a system
that for its brief era maintained itself
far from equilibrium (as, nearby,
seagulls and crows squabble over peanuts),
but that now lies splayed on asphalt, its fur slick
with last night's rain (rain is frequent here:
moss coats the stones), its matter returning
to the peace from which life flees and must flee.

Whatever. Listen: I do not serve death.

From the perspective of an emperor penguin chick, still in its down, upon the approach of the Terra Nova, 1911

> *"The whole incident was most interesting and full of suggestion as to the slow working of the brain of these queer people."*
> —"Uncle Bill" Wilson

Incisive minds, before they ever saw me,
guessed I must exist, then found me, here,
on the wrong ice, a derelict cut off
from colony and hope. They must suppose
I am awaiting still a long since past
migration. No. I know that I am dead
already, only Time has yet to choose
the means. And why not them? To die for truth—
even should Haeckel prove in error—that
is nobler than is granted most. (I think
of poor Adélies that exhaust themselves
in frantic circling: no, they never do
elude the seal's impending teeth.) The swell,
gnashing the floes, prevents approach, would carve
the ship to bits. Oh well. Nobility
in death is for the living. Why lament it,
Wilson? Say you cut me open, still
you would approach no closer to the fact.
You are allowed your guess, and glimpse. Past that,
the swell breaks angrily, the ice awaits.

The Cat is on the Mat

The rattle of metal coiled around metal, the bead spinning
Under the impulse of your thumb until, encountering
The wire's curve it's always just beside, it grinds
To a halt, this racket reminds you of some urgent
Task—what? You move to grasp it, but your hand
Ensnares itself in the metaphor that remains
Unmoored, and your thumb opposes your directive, fails
Or refuses to make contact with materiality, convinced
It can exist without its body. Maybe, just maybe
It can, maybe that's the ground of all its freedom, or maybe
This, too, is a fateful or fatuous error, born
Of doubt taken too far and now certain to hang
Over our thinking for centuries, until we rediscover
Pragmatism, the need to keep our bellies full, to get up
Off this couch and look 0, the cat, in the eye, saying
With purpose, with conviction, "I am here
For only this one day, this one hour, here
To feed you and to pat your head, and the moment I
Have completed that task, that's all, the whole arrangement
Will be disassembled and used to build even wilder
Scenarios, or tamer ones, or possibly a mix
Of both—it's so difficult to predict such things, in times
Like these. The time has come for me to lift myself
From this couch and say to you, 0, the thing I've been waiting
To say: *From the moment I arrived here, you must
Have known, you cannot not have known, that the hour
Was inexorably approaching when the clock would rouse
Itself to announce my scheduled departure, when I
Would begin to dismantle this fleeting assemblage, disconnect
The hand from the head, double check the water bowls
Are full, and for the last time scatter the lifeless
Parts of the whole that subsumed us. It's simple. Let me
Tell you. I only have to lift my left leg, reconfigure it
Such that my foot rests flat against the floor, then repeat
The procedure on the other side. Then I must raise
My torso, haltingly, to an upright position. Once this
Is done—we are nearing the end now—I must push
Myself, with one last burst, fully up to standing. That
Will set the whole of it in motion. That will make it go."

(Epicurus, you once described the gods)

Epicurus, you once described the gods
as open systems, atoms turning over
and over, but the form perpetual:
    fliessgleichgewichte.
Incessance their divinity, they hold
an infinite conversation with the void,
rapt in ataractic repetitions
    of give and take.
I like it, Epicurus, but it is shallow:
gods and atoms, nothing intervening.
It is good, but I know better—have
    you seen a person?
Have you seen that vortex, that profound churning
of cells, organelles, chemicals…? Yes, they must die,
but they are sacred: mortal gods nested
    in mortal gods.

Fleeing Ghost

for Paul Klee

As if your right hand, nothing more, unites
Your head to your emaciated frame,
As if your left hand clears away the proof
Of that exertion—angling to hide
Your fragmentation. (From?) But you are thin.
You find your flesh in fingerprints that dim
Your clarity to give you body. Lips.
But not your own. Possibly mine, my life
Fingering yours. So much to flee from, in
The dead hand past, the rest then taken on
At hazard. So you grasp across the gaps.
Yet—there it is, your skirt upturned: the tilt
That proves the dance. What you have fled, is gone.
The specter you threw off, that holds me still.

Fell

I have dreamed much: the slow drip
of thaw that rouses the snake
up from the numb earth; the zip

of the frenzied humming-bird
who, *for aught we know*, may blare
a furious song unheard,

unhearable with our ear;
and the hushed tree growing spare
with grieving. So fell the year.

But when the cold crisps the dirt,
and ice scabs the sleepy lake,
and life lulls—when only curt

crow-cackle still cleaves the air,
then I, at long last, will wake.

Anepikrita

I do not know you, Pyrrho, who you were,
the things you stood for, how you got along,
but let us for all that be friends. I've heard
the stories, how you would not halt for cliffs'
edges (your handlers scrambling to prevent
disaster), how you passed by Anaxarchus
trapped in the swamp (for which the guy forgave
and, hell, admired you), how you fled the dog
(so hard it is to cast the human off)—
but I know better than to trust the shrouds
of undecidable events. And I,
I cannot tell you all the times I've tripped
through inattention, missed the glaring (though
I guess you would rejoin that nothing's so),
nor all the times I've failed my friends, or cringed
in sudden, needless fear. They're all like that,
my recollections. I suppose you'd tell
me what absurdity it is to plague
myself this way with memory, mendacious
chronicler, and you'd be right. And yet…

I can't stop thinking of that word: the one
preserved third-hand, of doubtful origin,
and yet the nearest I can come to you.
It's tricky: *undecidable*. Suggests:
the fault in us, our judgment ill at ease
and always wavering. Or was your meaning
indeterminate? The fault in things
that natureless commit to no one form.
But now suppose (as I suppose you did)
they come to one, and fault lies everywhere—
what then? Time passes, and each trace of you
decays, and with each loss your substance shrinks
nearer to nothing. You become your name
and all detritus it has gathered: myths
so many mouths have spun, uncertainties
piled on uncertainties. And I know better

(do I?) than to trust them. What's this trust?
The stories miss their mark, but there's no mark
to miss, no Pyrrho to mistake, and who
you really were is neither here nor there.

And I? Am I a bloated label, too?
I call to mind all those I've pushed away,
material and irrefragable,
the unforgiveable forgotten crimes
that drove them off, inconstant for their substance:
the object, thrown in jest, that struck the head
with utter gravity; the talking over
to the point of tears; the casual
unthinking word that airborne bared its barbs—
how after this nothing could be the same.
What more is there to me than these, what more
but indeterminate desire? I want,
Pyrrho, a confidant. That could be you,
if friendship such as ours is not a figment,
if relations do not need relata.
Can need conjure its own satisfaction?
Maybe, or maybe not. I've no idea,
except for this: I'm lonely. Do I know
that friendship can fix love to empty space?
I do not know, but I maintain the search.

Nil mortalibus ardui est

Amid the rubble of a failed attempt
at order, nestled in the heap of dirt
and bricks and concrete, dull, its eyes pale blue,
a rat snake steals heat from the stinting sky.
Not much, I know: it's sluggish when I lift it,
and though I feel its latent power, still,
it hardly struggles. Rather—reconciled
too readily to this, as if it knows
(though it cannot, and even less assume)
that curiosity, not hunger, drives me—
it seems at peace with death, or maybe just
exhausted by this floating, fading world.

Row, Row, Row...

Its rabbit-ears prick up, tuned to the light
that's breaching the palpable sky. Shallowest
of flowers, the iris creeps across the water,
wavers. Look: how perfectly it mimics
its original.　　　　　　I say *original*
but only feel this breeze that's blowing now.
A silent picture hazarded in flux,
a reverie reflected in my face,
the iris now unsettles, now reforms.

Choose wisely

The tree—*there is no other way to say it*—
was growing *glass*, shards as of bottles smashed
in revelry deep-rooted in its trunk
and getting larger by the year.   Tell me,
too, of the concrete slab intussuscepted
at the base, the hungry roots *unhinging
like a snake's jaw* to swallow it, to make
a tree of gravel and sand.   Make sense for me
of the insect, long-departed, whose dust-brown husk
blends with the scar set in the dust-brown trunk.
Explain the hole through which the living thing
wriggled free. Where did it go? Where is it now?
What is left here?
                    Tell me what you know
of wounds and healing. Any word will do.

Mushrooms springing up in dampness

The coffee grinder is drowning out
the radio's nebulous voices. Snow
    falls: frivolous,
    widely spaced, melting
on impact. The barista listens
as a customer details
    the relative caliber
    of sundry fast-food coffees,
assigning each its proper grade.
Death is the end for which we are made.

Poem for John Ashbery

    All that… what was it? I don't know.
Some dusty thoughts, the glimmer of decay
enthralled by sudden sunlight, caught in play-
    ful, random, giddy dance, although
    the tendency is to a slow
indelible descent, to settle, gray,
on everything, as each mote drags the day
    closer to closing. Let them go.

    Driving digits through grime,
you scrawled a little drivel on the scrawl:
    details without detail.
    Your gift to famished time.
I'd like to rivet that lubricious fall.
    Like you, I'd like to fail.

Crane Collapse

The poem is a unity
governed by inner necessity.

Unsimple, unsolemn, frivolity
scattering the heartland, life

proceeds as, distant, Dorian
heckles the coastline, expends herself,

her indifferent rage blundering
its way north, toward Nova Scotia.

In Halifax, the hurricane
humiliates the imposed pride

of an erect crane, folds it in two
and allows it to fall on a nearby building.

Somewhere in Indiana, a man
thinks to himself, That is the poem:

an inorganic concatenation,
wrenched metal, shattered glass,

soldered in ruin by external
contingency, a chance meeting

become the prelude to rebuilding,
but someone else's, not my own.

Sprung

       Wait a minute, gentle Spring:
            do not yet come
laden with urgent pandemonium.
Before you get to slurring everything
    with rains that make mud of hard earth
    and draw out robins, wood-ears, leaves
to recrudescent struggle, let this dearth
remain a while to solace one who grieves.
Let one last caw recall her. Spring, give me
one day, one hour more of clarity.

    The dirt is crisp, a metal floor
             walled off by trees
like bars along the path. Patrolling these,
the guard keeps watch: abyssal eyes that bore
    through me to her and draw her out
    of me as I look back at them,
merging with her in vacuum-horror. But
then the crow blinks, and I'm again all him.
Dirt's dirt again, and trees mere trees. The spell
is broken. *No. I'm happy in my cell.*

    Only, face it, she is sprung.
          Death's ally, she
saved him the hassle, fled from—was it me?
to the old earth that once again is young.
    The letters fall like raindrops now
    on memory; now she is blurred
in my conceit, the mist that, thick and low,
I draw about her, tighter with each word.
Raucous and joyous, earth is moving on.
The crow takes flight in silence, and is gone.

Knowing better

Death is such a small thing, scarce present
in the crosswalk as you pass it, pause,
look back, its fractured form, not squirrel, no,
but goldfinch, splayed, half pavement now, and small.

We know better than to ask why: causes
will not satisfy, and we have long
given up on reasons. Just look. So small.

The large flattens the small. But platitude
will not do either, and we feel this, now
more than ever. Now, from this place, we
cannot accept less than shivered bone
itself, its hollows crushed. This becomes us.

The flies will be here soon to give us sense.
Stay here with me, for now, in senselessness.

Haibun

Felicity slumbers beside the Allegheny, nudged by tires, dock-floats, plastic bottles: a slowly shifting equilibrium model, meticulously emptied of time. Through it all, she sleeps, and so long as she sleeps, so long the river is silent, like an old film. Enter two young boys, decades apart in age, at just the same moment. And so the wrong register of language comes crashing back in, since no adults are here to maintain a semblance of order.

Waking to quizzical faces, Felicity is frightened. Quickly she remembers the adage: *it (the wild thing) is more afraid than you are.* Only they cannot agree on who, in this scenario, is wild. And so she shows the older boy the strands: how the river is really ink, and how the leaves are leaves. The other, as he watches, knows himself for an impostor and is branded "I".

Fingers dabbling in mud, I laugh to feel sense forming beneath them, laugh again to watch it vanish with the river's lapping—but nervously. *Vain man*, the river seems to say, slapping the mud. *Vain man*, titter the pages, twisting on their stems, straining, falling, sinking below the turbulent, formless words.

raking teeth through detritus, the river, threatening gestures

Tangled Weeds

Zhuang Zhou—who currently is writing this—
has got a toothache. Also (maybe) he
has lost himself. *Now where was I?* The tooth,
in which a pain has taken residence,
is still smarting, the brilliance of the gleam
reflecting off your slight smile distracting,
even now, in this moment of intense
focus. But night will fall, and even pain
must at some point go shopping, even pain
cannot subsist on nothing. *How are you?*
Zhou's trying now a new approach, no dice,
the pain is taciturn, the words no longer
come to it, not like they used to, back
in the days of exclamations, grimaces,
and other evocations. *Oh, that's right,
I had been busy, busy forgetting—what?*
Zhou looks perplexed, then—hastily (to Pain)—
*Oh, no, not you, don't worry, let's be friends,
given your plans to stick around, at least
for the time being.* But the time being,
just now arrived, has grabbed its coat: it must—
apologies—be off. How nervously
you swallow the moment, suck in air, the cool,
distant wind now flowing over the tooth,
yes, that one, and the mountains began walking,
the rivers began walking, clover blossoms
bursting in sky. The master gave a shout.

Detachment

warm sun shines forth

a particle riven from wind-etched stone
nudging aside the yielding grass

generals beyond the border

a head wandering far from its body
organs roving without direction

all word cut off

Poseidon facing Tantalos
in mutual incomprehension

oldsters sing their songs

at Pelops' grave the wanderer
last of the throng   taking his leave

Sonnet

Rain, meticulously around the edges
of perception tapping, massaging mosstones,
setting ripples swollen to interfering,
    coats you in quiet.

Fish, night-stippled, orange and white, are hoping,
just below the child who wants to know how
many bellies they would assuage, for something
    hidden here somewhere.

Where? You'd like to know. Underneath the lilies,
bursting half, half sere in their pond of fire?
Will you dive in after it? No? Why bother:
    sense arrives after.

Leave the garden. Go where the Giant Knotweed
    broadly awaits you.

"So priketh hem Nature in hir corages"

                The maple just
           beyond my window shakes
      with wind, shakes more with spring, the lust
           of birds whose chatter makes
    the earth seem, momentarily, a place
    more present than it really is, and wakes
           in me a stirring that my face
exposes briefly, swiftly hides, to gather dust.

                I look inside
           to watch the dust adrift
      on upslope flows, to see the dried
           up, ground down stirrings lift
    and fall haphazardly—oh, they purport
    to patterns, but get closer and they shift
           and twist away in dry retort:
The mind has mountains. So much cannot be denied.

                Pain?
           No: the din
      of echoes flung again
           and again off stone,
    and I feel the mountains grinding down
    beneath them, and… The maple in
           the front yard beckons: drown
these drought-born doubts in April's thudding rain.

Ephemera

     An *Iridopsis* drifting by
invents me, places me atop this stone
that jogs a glacial river. She alone
    is real, and I her thought, the dry
    remembrance of her complex eye
that now is turning—where cannot be known.
Stay. Stay. If you go, I am gone.

    Or else (I close my eyes) it's I
       who make the moth
        that with such trust
settles beside me. Does she, too, implore
    my whimsy for a moment more?

    Bubbles spin from froth to froth,
        and glaciers grind mountains to dust.

Sonnet

Take any word	FELICITY	will do
repeat it so	FELICITY	and soon the word
will vanish heard	FELICITY	and again heard
	FELICITY	so smooth so graceful you
glimmer	FELICITY	with double drift
the fitting word	FELICITY	you self-refer
as well the happiness	FELICITY	for her
who finds	FELICITY	your fitting gift
The moon	FELICITY	is beautiful
tonight and new	FELICITY	forgive that I
must leave	FELICITY	undone and dull
Are you still there	FELICITY	
	FELICITY	
	FELICITY	good-bye

(The bottlebrushes tongue the air)

The bottlebrushes tongue the air,
their flair a warm reminder how
your now-arriving reverie
will be co-opted, symbolized,
surprised by meanings off the cuff
and stuffed, no: crammed, no: glutted with
the pithy (pithy?) pithy tale
of alien sensation, maimed
by aimless jocularity—
will be, unfelt, fitted to rot.

Heraclitus

It's morning now: earth is awake,
At least this sliver that the sun,
New-made, enlightens. You watch its fire
Banish the dreamworld for more stable
Fantasies: for instance, this mountain
It's crowning: solid, long-standing, public.

But though the sunrise is a public
Possession, you watch it as if asleep,
As if it summits the dream of a mountain,
As if even the sun worships the moon
And its stolen light, taking as stable
Its monthly misgiving, the wavering water.

Let us linger over this water,
Encountered, as it is, only in private:
Always vanishing, never stable.
Every morning we awake
To the last remnants of the moon,
Too dim to show in that day's river.

You've misplaced yourself in this river,
Your heart consumed by its cold fire
And now dead ash. Meanwhile the moon
Cedes the sky to the sun; the public,
By now exuberantly awake,
Deafens; epiphany proves transient.

Slow down, slow down. That all is transient,
I allow. What of it? The mountain
Outlasts us: each day we awake
And it's there, inviting thoughts of the water
And wind that destroy it: slowly, a public
Spectacle, thanks to the tattletale sun.

You thought you had it, but no. The sun
Is sinking. Awareness recedes. The stable,

Cyclic sky reveals to the public
An old new face. Beside the river,
Streetlights cast globes on its murky water,
For whoever still can't fall asleep.

The moon watches itself in the river:
Transient disturbance, turbulent water—
But the laughter is private, the sliver asleep.

Flit

It is not given us to know. Life,
erratic as a butterfly's careening,
may yet prove to be an insect's dream.
Nothing so fragile, so unsteady as
the human mind—no better than the mushrooms
that in the morning poke from the earth, then vanish
before the moon can follow—can pretend
to certainty. No matter. We may still
proliferate hypotheses, and this
is good enough to hold at bay the fear
of gods and death. Consider: fire may
be motion, may be fluid—either way,
it is not Juno. I am dithering.

Enough. Here's how it might have happened. She—
No. Let me start again. Troy was on fire.
That's the key point. My city was on fire,
and its belly swarmed with Greeks. My terror sought
the release of hot blood on a cold blade,
but my mother pulled me back, against my will,
through streets unrecognizable, to a home
inexplicably intact. Anchises was there,
Creüsa, Iulus. I grabbed my son, my father,
told Creüsa to follow, a ways back.
Why? Why? I was still thinking of gore.
Let the fighting find me at the front, let her
hang back, where Death will not come looking. Stupid.
He has so many eyes, so many eyes
that sparkle with disdain, and I had none
to catch the flash that cut her down. Stupid.

Or it may have gone like this. Troy was on fire,
and swarming with Greeks. I grabbed my son, my father,
told Creüsa to follow, a ways back.
Why? Why? My mother, as she dragged me
through the streets I once knew, informed me
of my fate, of the wife, the faceless wife,

for whom I'd wage a war. Lavinia.
Then left me lamely standing in my home.
It's time to go. What else to say? *Dad, son,
with me.* But her, how could I face her, her
whom I would have to leave, if not now, soon?
And you, behind. Exactly so. She knew,
of course—not what, precisely, but, no less,
she knew and, knowing, she removed herself.
The streets as we fled furnished many weapons,
so true it is, that the dead will aid their own.

Darkness is often privation. The sun slinks
below the sea. The last rays of its radiant
cowardice fade, and we feel it gone all night.
But darkness may also be a presence, stinging
our eyes, our nostrils. Then the black sky
grows blacker, fed by an orange glow beneath.
And there is something that delights in flame,
that in its waking hours ever seeks
the conflagration conjured in its dreams.
And it is possible that as she ran
beside us, fled with us, a butterfly
enthralled her, drew first her eyes, then her legs
back, back, until she vanished in the smoke.

Maybe. Maybe. And a million maybes.
My feet I turned to Troy, my steps retraced.
Creüsa! No. *Creüsa!* No. Still no.
To the mountains, Iulus—she is gone.
All roads lead back to this unfractured fact,
thick and rich with being, like an atom.

Nothing Doing

A bare white wall descends, becomes a couch
(not mine, but temporarily residing
here) accumulating half-worn clothes,
an unused comforter, a shower curtain—
all things that might, together, tell a story,
only this is not a story, this
is someone's body sitting, doing nothing.

A dull bored thought ascends, becomes a self
(not mine, but temporarily residing
here) accumulating half-worn envy,
half-endorsed ideas, a narrative
that threatens to engulf it, make me real
for all its sitting, any glimpses I
have caught of Nothing, doing what it will.

Red Song

Anxieties unstartled, here I am,
    the wall before me white and blank
        but for this speck that stammers
blackly of the cosmos it encloses,
    ornament in which I watch,
        past icy rails that stretch
from wire fencing into endlessness,
    an ocean not itself, then sink
        beneath it, absent words
to mark the algal bloom's unnerving face,
    its vacant grin, its blood-red beard—
        just then, my vision crossed:
        the speck erased,
            the world lost.

Dialogue

      I cannot see you through
  this fog, and though I sense you're near,
I can't quite place you. Where are you, whose fear
        shakes your each word? And who?

            Fear? No, no, you've gotten it wrong: it's not that.
            Something else, but what? Even I'm uncertain,
            skeptical, a seeker myself in matters
                darksome as this is.

     What is it that you do
  each moment of existence, here
on this cold rock? Just wait for it to clear?
    That isn't, can't be true.

            Sadness, maybe, over the pain that outweighs
            pleasure, the dull ache that's the dominating
            presence on this vehement rock. It makes sense.
                Why am I cheerful?

     I just don't get it. How
is one to make sense of this blend
    of chill and beauty? How?

            That's the thing: I'm cheerful, I think, with equal
            reason, equal lack. This uneasy spinning
            captivates me. Marvelous in itself. Now,
                was I convincing?

     This spinning to no end,
this centrifuge— Where are you now?
    I'm asking for a friend.

            Friend, I'm still a seeker myself in matters
                darksome as this is.

Look, man, here's the thing…

You saw a rabbit in the moon. I never did.
You see that? That's its ear. But still the rabbit hid.

Soon you grew desperate. *Why won't you listen? Now,
it's got a carrot.* Nada. Crickets. Woof. Bow-wow.

Only it wasn't, as it happens, quite a dog.
A wolf? The rabbit-moon ran scared as you, agog,

juddered my shoulder. *Surely now…* Not now, not ever.
I fantasized about old Archimedes' lever—

I wanted to evict the moon, to yeet the rock
right out of orbit. It just hung there, shutterstock.

You took my hand to calm me. *Look, it doesn't matter,
not really, that you cannot hear the pitter-patter*

*of tiny rabbit feet across the vasty sky.
What matters is this moment now, together.* Why?

I wasn't buying it. That you would, with such ease,
give up your vision. *Come inside. You're gonna freeze.*

No. I clomped off, thudding, and my mind a muddle,
unwitting where I placed my feet, and then the puddle—

oh! I stopped to curse, and feel my socks soaked through,
my skin turned prune. I had to laugh—what else to do?

For here, now, bathing in the foot-fermented lake,
I see a bird. It cleans its feathers, gives a shake.

I part my lips to speak—no. No. I'm here alone.
The water settles and the moon returns to stone.

Canon

Like a water frog becoming a quail
or the tree outside now taking flight,
nothing is constant in the night
where even Change is growing stale.

Walk with me, love, along the trail
our walking carves, our footsteps light
like a water frog becoming a quail
or the tree outside now taking flight,

then part. This vividness will pale.
I know, because it has: I write
these lines too late to set us right,
dreaming of changes past the pale,
like a water frog becoming a quail.

Entering & Breaking

Oh, you rascal, you've been placing candles
On the backs of tortoises again,
Haven't you? It's been a while since
You last went plundering, and things are not,

Not quite, as you remembered, scurrying
In all directions as you try to prise
Them from their fixed accommodations, and
Now your whole sense of self is out of whack.

Calm down, will you? You only need to gather
Your thoughts, re-establish good relations—
Diplomacy, you know? A little tact
Goes a long way. This way the tortoise lights,

But now it's vanishing around the corner,
And it hits you: you are lost here, in
The furrows, too deep to get back out. That's when
You hear the worked-up owner: *Not again!*

Stalker

Heinz Chapel, Pittsburgh

The chapel seemed an enchanted
zone, suffused—I wanted to say—
with god instead of air. Outside, a sign
      stood guard, its bulletlike letters

admitting mourners only.
Inscrutably, this let me pass,
turning elsewhere to repeat the one message
      it could think to express.

Inside, the organ hushed.
It was time for words, for names, if names
can attach to dissipating things, that fracture
      into memories.

And so each storyteller
grasped their segment of the mammoth,
called it "mammoth", and tossed it on the heap
      behind the podium.

The heap remained a heap
of ungarbed bones. I turned to my neighbor,
but she could feel the proboscidean's
      hot breath condensing in

the chilly air around her.
I knew then why the place felt strange:
the room was full of minds made palpable
      by grief, the weight of each

pressing down, and down,
filling the empty, unfeeling space
I occupied, inhuman, cowering
      behind my bootleg eyes.

Pindaric

for Fernando Pessoa

Scuttling through the streetlit
streets of my exile, where I
still thrill and shrink to and from
the absences substantial
as atoms and as fictive,
I hear the shadows shifting
under the dim lights, singing:

singing through their layered grays
the dull tones of your vibrance,
scouring the sheets of your
anxiety until all
terror peels away and all
that remains is the tremor
of the animal alert:

Quiet, Bernardo.
The shadows possess you now.
It is time you lived.

On the bottom, in blue, a painted fish

From the bowl rise moths of steam to curl
around the desk lamp's bulb, the broth

shimmering as, livid over
nothing, I watch my anger swirl

in patternless patterns behind my clenched-
shut eyes. Digging through noodles, bok choy,

I seek out shards of silken doufu,
their plainness hidden out of mind.

(It appears crooked, that half-submerged)

It appears crooked, that half-submerged
    stick—but it is not.
How much mischief hides in that *appears,*
    how much more in that
is not. A whole world of confusion—
    no, two: the real one
and the apparent alike dwell there,
    by their requited
antipathy sustained. Stick, you are
    a trickster, wearing
now this face, now that, shrugging off each
    as the medium
demands. Now, you resemble a stick,
    straight (enough), hung half
in water, half air, tossing off light
    in patterns wholly
sensible, under such conditions.
    (Do I ask too much
of you, stick? You're only a stick. Still:
    no thoughts but in things.
Maybe better: *no things but in thoughts.*
    It comes to the same.)
My eye, unused to light in water,
    denies the water
though it sees it, certain: only air.
    Worlds the fruit of this
first disobedience, worlds that split
    you, stick, in two: real
and less than real, body and shadow.
    Do I ask too much
of you? But I ask only that you
    appear as you are,
and this you'd do without my asking.
    What is more (I trust,
stick, I am not boring you with all
    this babbling), I
have heard a most curious report.

I have heard: *no stick.*
I have heard: *no air, no water, no light, no things, no thoughts.*

Free-Floating Clouds

for Sam Francis

Or else what? The dripping of thirty faucets
banters of irregular hours (muddled
measure of a muddled idea), perplexing,
     slowly, our clamor.

"…if you catch my drift," but, arriving too late,
after snow has piled up and life lies buried
underneath the glistening cold, well, no, I
     never do catch it,

rather find myself in the thaw, unclenching
my stiff legs and piecing myself together—
badly. Pardon me. I'm still learning how to
     retrofit data.

Now the crows have settled, like homes erected
on misgiving ground, in the trees. They've started
cawing, densely now, now in isolation,
     certain of something

which, I will admit, is most likely true, but
which I find I can't disentangle from that
which most likely isn't. For instance, this caw,
     which is—both? neither?

Wait. I'm told my methods all lack sufficient
rigor, told my efforts to date are voided,
having been engorged by the sinkhole that I
     should've seen coming.

Nothing happens, nothing is settled—nothing,
though at least we get a few metaphoric
insights, maybe. Maybe all this will make sense
     later, I promise.

Frogs in Artificial Light

Along the confield's concrete rim
they're scattered, poisonous and poised,

watching the two fakes of the moon:
inert and distinct, diffuse and wavering.

Halogen columns crumble, godlike,
in wind, are replenenished by wind.

It's nearing, the hour when everything
eidetic must be left behind.

Rising, by the splash I learned
just what it was I would come to lack:

not fear, not misplaced prudence, but
the plunge, the swerve, the curving back.

Going

Stay gone! At night, above the Wabash,
    spiders string themselves between
        railing and streetlight, all abdomen,
            slinging the silent

geometry of hunger, daring
    the wind to undo their tethers.
        The wind strains, and fails, and stills,
            and is transfixed.

A butterfly lies dead at my feet,
    a ship careened. I hold it over
        the silent river, let it drop
            to its vessel's home.

You suspect… but incorrectly:
    featherlight, freely and easily
        I twist down the still air
            to mirrordark water.

Rose Novick is an assistant professor of philosophy at the University of Washington. She writes poetry as philosophy by other means, attempting to understand self and other, and perhaps to span the chasm between them. Or at least to fall in the leaping. Anything more about her you might wish to know, the writing itself will say, if it is sayable.

www.ingramcontent.com/pod-product-compliance
Lightning Source LLC
Chambersburg PA
CBHW031127160426
43192CB00008B/1136